# Miniature Schnauzers

by Julie Murray

Abdo Kids Jumbo is an Imprint of Abdo Kids
abdobooks.com

**abdobooks.com**

Published by Abdo Kids, a division of ABDO, P.O. Box 398166, Minneapolis, Minnesota 55439.

Printed in the United States of America, North Mankato, Minnesota.

102025

012026

Photo Credits: AdobeStock, Getty Images, Shutterstock, Thinkstock

Production Contributors: Teddy Borth, Jennie Forsberg, Grace Hansen
Design Contributors: Candice Keimig, Julia Line

Library of Congress Control Number: 2025936507

Publisher's Cataloging-in-Publication Data

Names: Murray, Julie, author.

Title: Miniature Schnauzers / by Julie Murray

Description: Minneapolis, Minnesota : Abdo Kids, 2026 | Series: Dogs | Includes online resources and index.

Identifiers: ISBN 9798384907527 (lib. bdg.) | ISBN 9798384908227 (ebook) | ISBN 9798384908579 (read-to-me ebook)

Subjects: LCSH: Miniature schnauzer--Juvenile literature. | Working dogs--Juvenile literature. | Dogs--Juvenile literature. | Dogs--Behavior--Juvenile literature. | Animal behavior--Juvenile literature.

Classification: DDC 636.7--dc23

# Table of Contents

## Miniature Schnauzer

Miniature Schnauzers are small dogs with big personalities. They are playful and smart. They are good family pets!

Miniature Schnauzers come from Germany. They were **bred** in the late 1800s to catch rats. They also helped guard farms and **herd** cattle.

Germany
Europe
Africa
N
S
E
W

Miniature Schnauzers have a **compact** body. They stand about 14 inches (35.6 cm) tall. They can weigh up to 20 pounds (9 kg).

Miniature Schnauzers have a thick coat with two layers. The outer coat is **wiry**, and the undercoat is soft. Their main coat colors are black, salt and pepper, and black and silver.

black
salt and pepper
black and silver

Their features give them a strong look. The dogs have a bearded **muzzle**. They also have deep-set eyes with bushy eyebrows.

Their ears naturally flop forward to form a *V* shape. Some Miniature Schnauzers have **cropped** ears that stand straight up.

## Grooming

Miniature Schnauzers have a double coat that requires regular grooming. Weekly brushing keeps their coat healthy. It is also important to clip their nails and clean their ears.

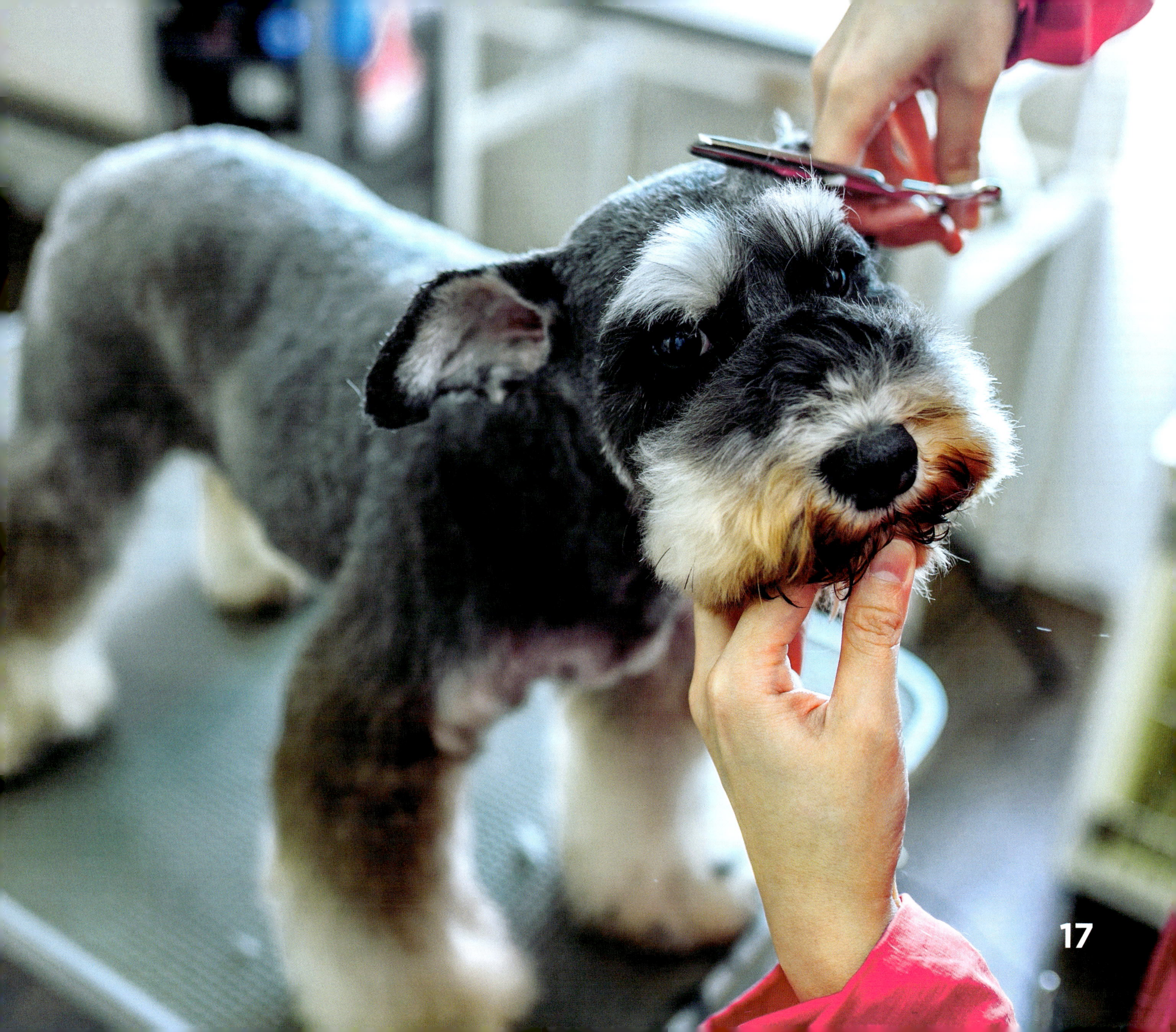

## Exercise

Miniature Schnauzers are active dogs that need daily exercise. They enjoy walks and playing fetch. They love having a space to run and play.

## Personality

Miniature Schnauzers are social dogs that do not like to be left alone for too long. They like to cuddle and be part of the family.

## More Facts

- Miniature Schnauzers want to please their owners and are easy to train. They do well in **agility** and **obedience** competitions.

- Miniature Schnauzers usually live 12 to 15 years.

- The American Kennel Club officially recognized the **breed** in 1926.

# Glossary

**agility** – a sport where handlers guide their dogs through a timed obstacle course.

**bred** – developed over time for a certain purpose.

**breed** – a particular type of animal.

**compact** – taking up a small amount of space.

**cropped** – made to stand straight up.

**herd** – to gather, lead, or drive a group of animals.

**muzzle** – the part of the head of some animals that contains the nose, jaws, and mouth.

**obedience** – having to do with the act of obeying.

**wiry** – like wire in being thin and strong.

# Index